SPIRITUAL UNFOLDMENT 3

SPIRITUAL UNFOLDMENT

3

*The Way to the Inner
Mysteries*

WHITE EAGLE

THE WHITE EAGLE PUBLISHING TRUST
NEW LANDS · LISS · HAMPSHIRE · ENGLAND

First published December 1987

British Library CIP data

White Eagle *(Spirit)*
Spiritual unfoldment.
3 : The way to the inner mysteries.
1. Spiritualism
I. Title
133.9'3   BF1311.W/

ISBN 0-85487-075-X

*Set in 12 on 14pt Linotron Baskerville by
Goodfellow & Egan Phototypesetting Ltd, Cambridge
and printed in Great Britain
at the University Printing House, Oxford
by David Stanford
Printer to the University*

CONTENTS

PREFACE

THE TALKS of which this book is made up
were given by White Eagle over quite a long
period of time. The earliest of them dates
from 1934, while others were given rela-
tively recently, so that a matter of some
thirty or forty years could separate them.
And yet, remarkably, the teaching remains
consistent throughout. Although what
White Eagle had to say evolved and grew as
we, the listeners, became readier to receive
and absorb his message, we do not know of
any instance where he corrected or contra-
dicted himself.

All the talks except one were given in the
places of worship of the White Eagle Lodge
in London or in Hampshire, England. At his
'Inner Teachings', as they were called, White
Eagle always began with an invocation to lift
the consciousness of his hearers out of the
everyday and to bring the co-operation of
the heavenly beings; and he never left us
without some form of blessing. Although

some rearrangement has been made to give unity to this book we have tried so far as possible to maintain this pattern.

Readers who want a mass of intellectual knowledge will not find this in White Eagle's books. White Eagle spoke from the heart to the heart. He spoke and speaks to the human heart of his listeners, spoke in answer to a very human need in the heart of each one. His way was, at the same time, gently to open little doors to inner knowledge, so that if we followed where he led we would see through to a deeper knowledge for ourselves. He always emphasized the need for service, to seek spiritual unfoldment not for ourselves or our own gain or spiritual advancement, but that we would be better healers – in the broadest sense of that term. And he taught that as we learnt to serve and to give truly through unfolding the inner awareness, so heavenly truth, knowledge of the divine mysteries, almost impossible to clothe in words, would be revealed to us, or to the aspirant on the path of spiritual unfoldment.

Readers for whom the book THE QUIET MIND is a constant companion may find the occasional passage which is familiar. We hope that you may enjoy seeing familiar sayings in their original context; indeed they may even take on a new and stronger meaning for you, seen in this light. A short passage from HEAL THYSELF also appears within the original talk. If this should inspire the reader to go back and study that book further we shall not think the repetition wasted.

Who is White Eagle, you may ask? We can only say that we know him as a wise, loving personality, still very close and real to all his world-wide 'family', who spoke to us from the inner world through the instrumentality of Grace Cooke while she was on earth. He never made any claims for himself, except just to say that he was a messenger, a spokesman for those greater than he in the world of light. 'Old White Eagle', he used to call himself. But to those of us who learnt from him, and were guided and cared for by him, he is a wise and loving teacher of golden stature, truly one of the 'elder brethren', and all love.

We believe that as you read his words with your heart as well as with your mind, you will be in close touch with him, and he will speak to your heart as he spoke to the hearts of his listeners in years past. His teaching remains as alive today as it was then.

Y.G.H.

1

THE ANCIENT MYSTERY SCHOOLS

Let us open our hearts to the Great Spirit of the universe. We worship, we praise, we would glorify Thy holy name and Thy creation. We learn to worship Thee as Father, Mother and Son, holy and blessed Trinity: three great principles of life. O Lord, we earnestly pray for a greater revelation of Thy truth, Thy love, Thy power. May these Thy children who come in search of truth have the blindfold removed from their eyes, so that they may see the light and be filled, and be united in spirit with their brethren on earth and their brethren in the world of spirit. May joy and love and peace unite us all.

Amen.

AGES AGO, when the present human cycle was in the process of birth, wise men, those we call 'God-men', came to this planet from worlds which had already evolved far beyond any spiritual growth conceivable by ourselves. These God-men brought knowledge of the ancient mysteries to the earth, they came here to establish schools of wisdom for the guidance of mankind. Temples were built wherein those who were ready were received and instructed, and learnt of the mysteries of life, the ancient wisdom.

They were taught from the invisible worlds also. Remember, all that manifests on earth is first born from the invisible, and comes through later into physical, or outer manifestation. So in these schools of learning or of light the mysteries of life, even before manifest on earth, were studied in reverence and awe.

To this day, in the secret places of the earth, tablets of stone can be found upon which this ancient knowledge is inscribed in symbol; relics hidden in the mountains, in caves or temples. Such records are also imprinted on the ether, and are called the etheric or akashic records, to be read only by initiates, those who are ready.

Today all are free to seek the mysteries. Once a man or a woman longs for wisdom, not out of curiosity, or to satisfy a greedy mind, or for his or her own satisfaction, but rather that he or she may serve, then they set their feet upon a path which leads ultimately to enlightenment. When a soul through this great longing and searching finds his or her path, then teaching and guidance come from the invisible. Having found his or her path the soul should remain true to it, be true to the inner light. Follow the one, avoid the many, be true to your inner light, and the mysteries of the invisible worlds will be revealed to you in the degree that you are ready and will use the knowledge thus attained in selfless service. And remember, service can take many forms. You are not bound to this or that particular form of service, but you should obey the guidance of your heart.

The mystery schools of the past served a great purpose in revealing the eternal life of the spirit. They showed man his origin and destiny, where he came from, why he is on earth and what is his goal. But there came a time when mankind became deeply im-mersed in physical matter; he lost the use of that 'third eye' which reveals the spiritual worlds. Deterioration set in and there was a misuse of spiritual power – due perhaps to

———

young priests becoming too eager and admitting students unable to stand up to the testing. Yet none of this was outside the divine plan, for man had to develop both physically and mentally. He had to become 'earthed'; his will had to be developed and become strong.

And so the masters of wisdom withdrew, and departed into the secret places of the earth, where they still dwell. Yet, from time to time, from the Temples of the Ancient Wisdom a teacher comes forth who presents the truth once more to humanity. Particularly is this so at the beginning of any new age, as humanity moves forward into a new way of life and thought. At such times there comes always a restatement of ancient and eternal wisdom, in a form suitable to that new age, and to help humanity through the difficult transition from one age to another.

We are now on the cusp of a new age, the age of spirit, of the air, of the mind and thought power, and great new knowledge awaits mankind when men are ready to use it with wisdom and love. This is a time of wonderful revelation. The heavens are opening and the invisible hosts are working amongst men; the light is slowly permeating

---

the minds of humanity. But before the greater revelation can come, mankind has much work to do upon itself. Men and women must become more receptive to spiritual truth, more spiritual in their attitude to life. The Christ within must be encouraged to grow and take possession of heart and mind. Intellect and intuition must work together in harmony. There is much for all to learn, but the foundation of all spiritual learning must be brotherly love.

But brethren, *there is no short cut*. There is a difference between, on the one hand, speeding up spiritual evolution, and on the other trying to take a short cut to heaven. The first is possible – indeed, the opportunity to do so is now presented to mankind; but the second is not possible. On the spiritual path there can be no short cuts. Every lesson has to be thoroughly absorbed and put into practice. But with the baptism of light now pouring upon the earth, those who have earned the opportunity will be able to make a big stride forward. You have already noticed the many groups that have been formed and the opportunity which is being given to the masses, and will be given increasingly, to learn about their latent spiritual powers. Hitherto only those who entered the mystery schools could qualify for this knowledge, and secrets were kept from the masses. Now, in this new age of Aquarius, the gate of initiation is being opened wide to all – but herein lies danger. Humanity has to learn to discriminate and discern between the false and the true.

Numbers will be drawn into brotherhood groups to develop the light within, which gives the true power to heal the sick and to reach out to the soul of a brother or a sister. This light, generated in the course of spiritual unfoldment, is very real; it radiates from the pupil and penetrates the soul of another. But this is a sacred power and must be used with delicacy, with love, with discrimination and discernment. This is why it has remained secret from the masses. But the whole of mankind now has advanced to the point when it may have access to spiritual knowledge.

We urge you to strive for discernment and discrimination in selecting your path of unfoldment, because teachers will arise, with limited knowledge, who will sweep some off their course by their outpouring of words. Words have their place and can open doors in the mind, but you cannot advance into the temple of initiation on words alone. The passwords on the spiritual plane are sounded not by words only, but in the heart. The surest indication of true teaching is an innate and pure simplicity, and yet, beneath, a profundity. Always look for simplicity first in any revelation which may come to you. Then diligently put into practice the truth you have found, being and becoming the beautiful truths revealed, so that you *live* them.

Many of you who read our words were once workers in brotherhoods in the past, particularly those who now serve in some new-age group or centre of spiritual light. Those drawn to such service have already gained knowledge of certain truths through experience and service in past lives. Though the physical life-span ends, and even the personality which survived death is at length laid aside – or, shall we say, is hung up in the 'wardrobe' above, there to wait until again required – the inner wisdom once learned is never lost. That is why many of you feel again the call of the ancient wisdom within your breast. You need no convincing, you *know*, the truth remains within you, built into your soul. Perhaps at one time you failed, you turned away from the path; but there is no disgrace in this, so long as you try again. God is loving and you are offered fresh opportunity with each successive life. So even when you fail in your tests, go forward with courage, inspired to fresh effort, determined to do better when the next opportunity comes. Above all, remain true.

The temple training of old, the enforced seclusion and isolation, is no more. Today the pupil is no longer shielded from temptation, but lives in the world, subject to the continual pull of the lower mind, of the excitements and passions of physical life. Of old, the student withdrew, quietly pursued the path, worked diligently, serving and healing; and powers came which drew aside the veil between this and the invisible worlds. These powers can be yours today, too, but you have first to battle in the field of life, and in doing so learn to discriminate between the false and the true, the real and the unreal, the important and the unimportant.

There are three major steps of initiation into the mystery schools. The first is that of the neophyte, the learner. When he first sets forth upon the path, the neophyte attracts the attention of the great ones. They hear his cry for knowledge, recognize his longing to be of use to God and to the masters, to be worthy of service, and so he is accepted as a pupil. Then comes the process of purification. The higher vehicles or bodies of man need much cleansing, much purification, because much has been gathered into them which hinders and obstructs his vision, his understanding. Therefore episodes of trouble, sickness and suffering may come; some may be born with a crippled body, endure great tragedy, possibly even commit crime: but, remember, these may be the soul's own choice, so that it can be purged, prepared, purified, made ready to receive and to serve.

The next step, the second degree, is that of the disciple. The disciple learns implicit obedience to the master, and to be exact and precise in all his working, because for the true craftsman there can be no slipshod methods. He learns to work upon himself, shaping and perfecting that which before was frail and weak. The disciple learns to listen to the voice of the master, the Christ within his own breast; and the Master, his own master, teaches him wisdom and shows him the way of life. He may deceive none, not even himself, for deception there cannot be in the second degree.

The third degree is when the disciple is ready to receive illumination, when he can be trusted with the secrets of the inner mysteries. He must be able to function on the invisible planes without hindrance or limitation, for it is in these inner worlds that true initiation takes place. Then indeed the initiate is touched by the master's hand and raised to a 'sublime degree'; he is raised from the grave of materialism and delusion, the corruption of earth, and born again into the true light of his heavenly home.

Thus do the Brothers of the Light work on, purged of all base desire. They are the white-robed, crowned with illumination; yet truly simple and with deep humility, knowing that all attainment, all that has been won by self-conquest and renunciation, comes from God, and not for their own glory or aggrandisement. As true and perfected brethren they lay all before the Great Architect of the Universe, to be used in the service of humanity.

———

◎◎

2

'WHEN YOU HAVE SET YOUR FEET UPON THE PATH . . .'

We wait in the stillness of the spirit to receive the spiritual outpouring from the centres of Love, Wisdom and Power. We resign ourselves to the light of Christ . . .

IN THE process of his evolution man has long concentrated upon self as he journeys upward – and necessarily so. He had to become self-conscious; but self-conscious-ness will give place in time to God-consciousness, and this has three main modes of expression – power, wisdom and love.

Many today long to find a way of service, so that they can help to relieve suffering, and help the younger brethren towards har-mony and happiness. The path is not easy to find at first, and being found, is difficult to walk steadfastly. There is so much to confuse

---

the aspirant, and when he has found his path, so much to draw him off it.

You may ask, 'How is the path to be found?' First by entering the chamber within, and praying for wisdom. When presently the light comes, it will not be due to any mental stimulation, but will be born from the heart.

How is the soul ensnared in the entanglements of mind and body ever to find this inner light and then be sure that it has found truth? One thing is essential – purity of life. What do we mean by this? Asceticism? A withdrawal from contact with all worldliness? No; for we have now reached the next spiral of evolution, and the aspirant today is not concerned with a monastic or ascetic life as of old, but is rather called to mix with humanity, to carry light into the world and into the minds of all those he or she encounters. It is this light, burning brightly in the man or woman, which brings healing and comfort. By purity we mean purity of all the vehicles, or bodies – the mental body (the thinking body), the desire body (the feeling body), and of course the physical body.

Thus the neophytes of old had first to learn how to live purely – to purify the physical body for service by correct eating and drinking, by daily ablution and physical discipline; to purify the mental and emotional bodies through prayer and meditation. They were also taught how, through meditation, they could call upon the great angels of the elements to bring to the soul and to the physical body the life-forces which exist in those elements. The brothers in those days lived to a great age because they had learnt the inner secrets of nature, and they had also been trained in godliness. Godliness is eternal life. They learnt also how to serve correctly and perfectly; their teachers were kind but they were strict, and brethren had to be obedient. Obedience was one of the first and most important lessons for the apprentice then, as now. The outworking of the law of karma was demonstrated practically to them in their daily lives; they found that if they broke the Law they suffered in some way. Thus they came to realize the importance of obedience and self-discipline.

Now, this training which the brethren of those days had to undergo on the outer plane, you, although you do not realize it, are going through now in your physical life. So many live in ignorance of the true

---

purpose of their lives, but when you have even a little knowledge of what your experiences are doing for you, my brethren, you will be so happy and thankful, and live joyously. As you work sincerely and conscientiously in your inner life and in your daily round, you are purifying your body and mind and stimulating your spirit; by your work your whole being is gradually becoming illumined. For as a soul lives in close proximity to its Creator, so, more and more, is it absorbing the essence of divine life and becoming a perfected soul – man made perfect.

When the pupil first sets out on the path, he loves, he wants to offer himself in service. Now every spiritual art is developed and strengthened by service. The very love which causes a man to want to give, to serve God and his fellows, is, as it were, the sparking plug which sets his soul alight. Love is the key to the whole of life. Love is the life-giving creative power.

Whole-hearted desire to develop his spiritual powers so that the light of the Great White Spirit may shine through him to serve mankind is a most beautiful state of mind for man to achieve. All gifts of the spirit can be of the greatest service to humanity and can be embodied in one word – healing. If, for instance, you develop clairvoyance, or clear seeing, it really means that you develop the gift of seeing into the innermost part of all life, into the innermost centre of spirit of your brother man, into the centre and the beginning of life – God, the Alpha and Omega. Once you have made this contact, if only for a flash, you are henceforth a channel, for you have opened the way for the creative power and light to flow into you.

True spiritual development comes from within you, from the spirit, from the jewel within the lotus of the heart. When that jewel, which is the Christ Spirit, the tiny seed of the God life planted in you, starts to develop, your whole being in time becomes flooded with light, and this brings a healing power which will radiate from you wherever you go.

Sometimes it seems, when you have set your feet on the spiritual path, that you immediately encounter every possible difficulty and frustration. What are you going to do? Are you going to kick out? Are you going to turn and run away? Or are you going to deal with every situation which arises, sensibly, and by the light of Christ in you? We are talking to you in your own language, but we are speaking truth. People so often say, 'Oh, White Eagle, White Eagle, why did this happen to me? What have I done to deserve this?' We hear and understand the human cry but, beloved children, we can only assure you that what seems to you to be a tragedy will eventually reveal itself as a wonderful opportunity for you to learn, and to develop those spiritual faculties which will eventually remove you from all the anguish, the frustration, the hurts and disappointments of physical life. A soul can only learn these lessons through life on earth. You have to learn to accept what is given to you to bring forth the God in you, so that you deal with life in a godly way. And remember, the angels are ever ready to help you.

We hold before you the life of the Master Jesus: such a simple, pure, holy life, a demonstration of how life ought to be lived in the physical body; a life of sacrifice and service, a life of love – but a life in which he had to be strong too. Don't think that to love means to be easy-going and soft. There are times when you have to grip a situation with courage and determination, and with trust and faith in the Great White Spirit; and as you do these things, really living the life, so you are developing your spiritual gifts, and so you will become a perfect seer, a perfect listener, a perfect server.

May the Great White Spirit bless you all and give you peace . . .

———

3

THE 'I' AND THE 'NOT I'

Almighty heavenly Father, we meet together in unity of spirit, in brotherly love, aspiring to the spiritual realms of wisdom. May we all learn something of Thy truth, and carry forth into the world of action the will and the power to express in human life the beauty which we shall find in communion with the Spirit.

Amen.

YOU HAVE often heard us say that it is not enough to search records and books for knowledge. You may read whole libraries, but mental knowledge, of itself, will not take you very far on the path to the eternal light. There is but one way to find the path and to walk that path when you have found it, and this is by your own inner experience, and by work in your daily life. Words, my brethren, are of little ultimate avail to the disciple. It is in action – the daily striving, the periods of meditation, the putting aside of everything which does not belong to the real you, that development comes.

In the mystery schools of the past the pupil was led by his guide to the door of the temple of wisdom. He knocked (do you remember the words of the beloved Master, *Seek and ye shall find, knock and the door shall be opened unto you?*) and sought admittance to the temple, where he was tested very severely before he could proceed. Today, you also knock upon the door – not physically but in your spirit. Something in your heart stirs. You long for wisdom, for understanding: you long to serve, and to know how you may serve. The Master hears your cry, and you are accepted as a pupil – and then the testing comes. You are almost daily confronted by the tests which your higher self has sought, but which the outer self, in ignorance, rejects and grumbles at.

The real you, the soul which is stirring, awakening, searching, has asked that you may be tested, that all manner of difficulties should fall across your path. In the trials that beset you always remember that your higher consciousness has asked for the light, is seeking initiation. The first awakening

---

comes when the soul realizes that it has the choice between good and evil. Then, the crying need when it knocks again at the door of the temple is for light. It cries out for light so that it can see the path before it. It comes in utter darkness, bound by the material world, and cries out for light. So the man enters, and after being put through certain tests is given what his soul longs for: the light is awakened within him, so that he dimly sees his place in the great plan, and is permitted to catch a fleeting vision of the light towards which he journeys. Faint at first, it sheds, a ray, and other wayfarers who meet him on the path, who also have been through that testing, recognize his light, as he too sees theirs. The elder brethren, when they look down upon earth as though looking into a dark night, see little lights twinkling like stars; these are they in whom the light has been kindled, and you, no doubt, are numbered among them.

Immediately a man sets forth on his quest, passes his test and shows forth the little gleam of light, then the teacher comes. The light is a signal to the masters, to the teachers, and to those angel beings who watch the destinies of humanity; they know the need of the child of God, and they come to assist the spirit within to become stronger, brighter, to bring the whole being towards perfection.

Beloved children, sometimes the little light waxes strong; sometimes it flickers till it seems almost as though it might go out altogether, but this it never does. It is buffeted sometimes, and the heart within the brother or sister grows weak; but as we watch, we fan the flame, and try to give strength and courage to the pilgrim on his way. And remember that although we speak from the spirit realms, we too are walking the path, and we too have walked over the roughest stones, even as you have, and as you are still doing. The path is no easier for one than another. All must tread the same road, the road of daily sacrifice, daily putting self a little more on one side, daily resisting the temptations of the lower self. Do not think that your task is any harder than that of those who have gone before, for all have trod the self-same road.

Now, many parts go to make up man– woman, and there are many aspects of yourself which you think are *you*, but which are not you at all. You know (although you do not always remember) that you are not your body, that your physical body is not the whole of you – just your clothing, or your 'working tool'. You say, 'I am spirit; I live after my body has been laid aside'. There are other aspects of your being, too, which survive physical death, but they are still not the real you. There are the emotions, passions, selfish desires; and these belong, not to your spirit, but to your mind, to your astral body, your desire body. They are not the real 'I'; they too are transient, and in the end will die away, even as your physical body is laid aside. But beyond and beneath all these there still remains the real 'I', the Son of God, the light, your eternal self. You can stand aside from all the facets of the 'not self' and analyse them. But you cannot stand aside from the real self, the 'I', the Son of God, the light. There is within you the real 'I', the Will, the divine spark, which should control the whole self, but usually souls allow themselves to be bound and ruled by the 'not I' and all the chaos around them.*

We suggest that you spend some time

*The term 'the not I', should be distinguished here from the term that is used, with a different meaning, in Jungian analysis.

each day trying to recognize and quietly lay aside the various outer layers, the physical, astral, mental and emotional, until you find this real 'I', the eternal self.

On the one hand are all the worries, the fears, the angers, the foolishnesses, the desires – all these are the 'not I'. On the other, 'I' stands poised, polarized, still . . . the spirit, the light within.

Give the 'I' every opportunity in this daily meditation to become stronger, a polarized light . . . and understand that the 'I' that you identify in meditation is the real you – a God in embryo. It will never lead you off the path, never lead you astray . . .

The sorrows, the responsibilities, the anxieties which you think are yours, do not belong to you at all. *You* are that shining self, that light, that essence of being that you find in the hours of meditation.

All your will to do good lies with the 'I'. 'I *will* to do good, to do God's work, to put egotism aside, to deny the claims of the "not I".' The reason why so many fail to see the light is because they are so closed, so wrapped up in the 'not I'. But the Christ light burning within, willing you to do that which is good in the sight of God and putting aside all egotism, also reveals to you the same light in others.

Man was created in God's own image; the conception of the Perfect One is within the Trinity, is part of God. And you, my brother, my sister, *you* are that perfect conception of the child or son of God held within the mind of the Father–Mother. Meditate on this, upon the holy three – God the Father, God the Mother, and *you*, the child . . . the very child of God, an aspect of that Trinity.

If, each day, you aspire to become in tune with the infinite, you will be developing the child of God, the Christ child in your heart. Men so sorely need that closer relationship with the source of all life, the Father–Mother God, and when man's life on earth is built on an understanding of this relationship of child and parent, man and God, there will be no more suffering and sickness, chaos and war.

Now we will unite, beloved children, in thanksgiving to the Great White Spirit . . . .

May Thy peace, the peace of love, abide with us for ever.

———

◉◉

⊚⊚

4

BODY, SOUL AND SPIRIT

---

*Let us be still and seek the silence of the spirit
deep within . . . and there may we hold perfect
communion with the angels who praise and
glorify their Creator.*

*O God our Father, we pray in deep humility
that Thy spirit may speak to our waiting souls;
may the fire of Thy life grow in power and
radiance in our hearts.*

Amen.

BY OPENING your souls to divine love you will
release yourselves from all strain, and ten-
sion will be relaxed. We come with great
brotherly love to commune with you, bringing with us many companions of your spirit;
we pray that these companions may become
very real to you – and not only discarnate
human brethren, but also the angels who are
all about you. May you be conscious of their
ministry, and of the light which shines from

---

them: such a light as never before, shining in your heaven.

Let us turn now to the three worlds of man's being. Many are the terms used to refer to the unseen planes and to man's subtler bodies, and a good deal of confusion exists as to the meaning of the words 'soul' and 'spirit'. Now while he is on earth, man is a threefold being consisting of body, soul and spirit. Each of these worlds or aspects bears its relationship to the divine triangle of power, wisdom and love. Within the body of man is to be found expressed the profound mystery of the universe. Usually, man while in incarnation regards his body as all-important, and finds it difficult to become detached from it. After all, it is through this vehicle that all his experiences of life come, and his body therefore represents for him sorrow or happiness, pain or joy, and all the emotions and feelings experienced by the man while on earth.

In the great mystery schools of the past the human body was the first study for the neophyte. Pictures and models of it were displayed in the inner temples, with each part or function related to some sign of the zodiac. The astrological or astronomical knowledge of the teachers and priests helped the pupil to understand and respond to the cosmic powers directed upon him. Through acquiring such knowledge, the man began to understand true healing, and to recognize the stellar influences which affected him while on earth. And he was shown that through the experiences of his earth life he was gradually gaining mastery of matter and of the physical body. He was developing the *power* aspect of his nature. Through many, many incarnations the creative power of God grows within the child of God. At first man uses for selfish purposes the power he is gaining, but ultimately, he uses them to the glory of God. He first becomes self-conscious, then God-conscious.

Together with the influences of the zodiac upon man's soul, the candidate learnt about the seven sacred centres in his etheric body (a close replica of his physical body), which lie concealed beneath the ductless glands; and that each centre was connected with or bore a relationship to one of the seven planets. So man responds to both planetary and zodiacal influences during physical life, both influences being concerned with his evolution and development towards perfection. Man's freewill is God's precious gift to him; through action of his freewill man eventually learns to discriminate between that which is good, or positive, and that which is evil, or negative.

This brings us to the second aspect of man's being, his soul, for in his physical life and through using this precious gift of will, freewill, he is learning to discriminate, to select the material which creates his soul life, his soul body. Don't think of the soul as something separate and apart from the physical life, or the soul life as a state to which we shall pass with the death of the physical body, for you live in a soul world *now*, and you are selecting now, through your own freewill choice, the material being built into your soul home in the world of spirit.

You speak of spirit people, living in the spirit world, but really they are better described as 'soul people', living in a soul world. In the world beyond, we find conditions made manifest and actual which have previously been created, and which are being continually created by the thoughts and desires and emotions of man during the physical life. This soul world and those who live in it are not far away somewhere 'up there' but all around you now.

We have said many times that as man is today, so will he be after death. Thus, if in daily life you build pure and beautiful substance into the soul body, then when the time comes you are released into a world of beauty and light, clothed in a body of light. There are very beautiful homes 'over there', but these are not always waiting and ready immediately the soul is released. If a person lives hampered by pessimism, heaviness, darkness and resentment towards life, conditions and people, so in the beyond he will wake to similar conditions – yet sustained always by loving companions of his spirit and by the guidance of his will, the divine Spirit within him, ever urging him onward and upward. A man's quality of soul is born of the experiences garnered through many lives on earth; thus, when reincarnating, the soul brings back into physical life soul qualities acquired in previous physical existences.

Kindliness and love are the two great attributes which draw to the soul the more beautiful substance; and therefore the soul body that becomes sensitive, beautiful, refined, will necessarily vibrate and respond

---

to a beauty in the next world to which a coarser soul substance cannot possibly react. When a man avows to live in love instead of hate, kindliness instead of cruelty, refinement instead of crudity, his soul substance too is refined, through purified emotions and desires.

The soul body is the temple referred to by seers and sages and prophets of old, the temple 'not built with hands', but by thought, aspiration and effort by the master mason, the divine Spirit, working upon the rough ashlar of the physical life and experience.

We have dealt with body, and with soul; what then do we mean by spirit? *No man hath seen God*, nor yet the spirit. Man can conceive of soul, and even that purified body which can become a temple of the spirit, but spirit he cannot see. Spirit is the divine urge, the God in man. It speaks to him through his heart. Ancient wisdom states that the home and seat of the divine Spirit is in man's heart. Actually, in the heart dwell seven seats – the 'seven angels round the throne' spoken of by St John; for within the physical life, within the physical body of man, is contained the whole universe, and the angelic beings, the lords of creation, the planetary angels, all find representation in the physical body of man. The whole mechanism of man's life on earth and in the soul world is fired – the only word we can find – by the divine Spirit which works throughout man's whole life, from lowest to highest, eventually to create or complete the master man, man made perfect. The divine Spirit radiates through, works in perfect harmony with, man's body and soul. The master man does not ill-use his physical body, but enhances its beauty by harmonious living. He does not defile it by wrong thinking or by injudicious feeding, but respects both body and soul, and thereby glorifies the divine Spirit, God, within him and without. From the divine he comes as pure spirit; from the divine we are born. The God from whom we come is our true home. And we too have been given the power to create and to become the perfect Son–Daughter which God our Father holds eternally in His heart, as the quest and aim of all creation.

Deep peace of the open prairie and the wind-swept sky, the flowing rivers, the quiet valleys and the noble trees standing stalwart and true on the mountain side, steady through all the boisterous

———

winds of life . . . deep peace of God dwell within us, giving us a like strength, to bring us back to Thee, our Father.

Amen.

5

THOUGHT-POWER IN SERVICE

Let us hold communion, raising our thoughts, opening our vision to the light and glory of God our Father . . . O Gracious Spirit, who hath given us life and in whom we live and have our being, may a ray of Thy glory find entrance into our waiting souls. We thank Thee for life itself, and for all the happiness which blesses our days. May we also learn through experience to thank Thee for our sorrows and our suffering, for joy and pain are alike in Thy sight. So may we receive understanding, and become more perfectly equipped for Thy service in the grand plan of evolution.

We would rest in Thy love and wisdom, now and at all times.

Amen.

WE ENFOLD you in loving understanding, brethren, for we see that sometimes you feel sorry and regretful, feeling that you have failed in some test with which you have been confronted, or when you have tried so hard and anxiously to give loving service. Don't dwell on such thoughts – banish them from your mind, but just resolve to do better next time. And if you do fail, or think you have failed, thank God for the elder brother who waits by your side, who understands and loves you and will help you to do better next time. He prays that his love may help you to become a finer instrument.

We are all as children. You live on earth, and are subject to many physical limitations; we, freed from the bondage of earth, may have a little more experience than you have, and surely, surely there are those above as far removed from ourselves as the earth from the farthest star! Yet we are all brethren, dear ones; we are all travelling the same path towards the infinite wisdom and love. What we have learnt we give to you, and what you learn you pass on to others who may be coming up the path behind you. Only do your best with the material which has been given you – the angels themselves can do no more.

We spoke earlier of the soul temple which each one is building while in incarnation. Now, one of the most powerful tools with which to work upon ourselves, and upon the soul temple we are all building, is thought. Although in days to come man will be principally concerned with the unfolding of higher or spiritual aspects of himself, at the present time he is largely concerned with the development of his mind, his mental qualities. In spite of this, so few people take heed as to *how* they think; they think at random, letting their thoughts tumble and jumble along together until their minds become like rag-bags, full of all sorts of queer odds and ends. Only occasionally does one meet a mind beautifully arranged, with all its contents neatly in order and under the control of the spirit.

Once we begin to understand the power of thought, we can use thoughts to shape our lives to beauty and harmony. Now we do not advocate 'self first' as an incentive to right thinking (indeed, to think first of self is anything but right thinking) but rather emphasize how you can help others and bless those around you by your right thought, your good thought. This should be the motive behind all your effort to think rightly. Nevertheless, you cannot send forth

---

good, kind and constructive thought, without reaping the harvest of the thought-seeds you have sown. So you may be serving a double purpose when you train yourself to think kindly and constructively. For this is the law of karma: man cannot escape harvesting the result of his thoughts. This is a serious consideration, for so few have any idea of the effect of their thoughts on others, whether those thoughts are directed personally or to the world at large.

We see that you sometimes worry about so-called infectious diseases, and what you call 'germs', or an infection by virus — but have you ever thought of the possibility of an infection by thought-forces? For if a person is inclined to shallow thinking or uncontrolled, undisciplined thought, he can prove receptive to negative forces of the astral plane, and will likely catch a 'thought-germ' which will trouble his etheric body and eventually find its way into his bloodstream, lessening his power of resistance to physical complaints. There is great truth in the teaching of Christian Science, for the continual thought of good, of God, enfolds a person in the light of Christ as in a protective armour. Those practising Science wisely, truly, will reap blessing not only for themselves but for others.

Thoughts can literally take shape, and are visible at the particular level to which they are attuned. For instance, thoughts of devotion ascend to the celestial plane, and create beautiful form at that level, while those functioning only on the astral plane would not register. Every thought which goes forth from you is seeking by the law of attraction some corresponding thought-vibration in the ether. Sometimes you say, 'Oh! I have a little black dog on my back'. Perhaps this is so, but it is a form of your own creation, and it is you who have chained it in position! On the other hand angry and critical thoughts can suffuse the astral and emotional body with the ugliest of colours which flash forth, flame-like, pointed and wounding. Let us have none of this sort of thinking! But rather choose for your companions bright radiant forms of thought, ready to serve both yourself and those around you.

Here is a way of service open to all. When you are in a public place – let us say, using public transport – watch, and note when someone enters the train or bus looking sad,

---

tired and depressed, or sometimes indeed very cross. Sit quietly sending forth love and peace to that person; try to imagine the kind of thoughts the Master would send to that poor soul. A well-formed and directed thought of love and kindness and light will find its mark, and you will notice that your neighbour will brighten. You will have helped him, so that his troubles will start to recede and he will perhaps even take on what you call a 'new lease of life' from that moment.

There are struggling human souls, many, like yourselves, earnestly endeavouring to overcome inner weaknesses which in their own souls they acknowledge. You cannot see or know the inner struggles of another, nor the difficulties and weaknesses which bind him and sometimes make him act in a way you do not understand; but you who are now learning, not only from our words but from the promptings of your own teacher, can do so much to help others by your kindly positive thoughts, by seeing the Christ in them. Think of your neighbour as being a child of God, as you are yourself, with the same problems that you suffer, the same weaknesses, the same aspirations.

Where this or that man stands, only God can know. Nevertheless, all are of the same spirit, and all experience the same struggles and problems and needs as yourself.

So go about life condemning none, but looking kindly and with love upon all; hold no harsh thought even about a so-called enemy. In truth, no man can really be your enemy, all are your teachers; and when you are tempted to feel injured or resentful because of some apparent injustice, look first within yourself and ask, 'What has this to show me, what have I to learn from this?' In time truth will reveal itself, so that instead of thinking antagonistically you will be able to say, 'Thank you, brother, for you have taught me much, and helped me'. The other person's motive is not your business. Behind is the guiding hand of wisdom. The great lords of karma rule your ways, and any apparent injustice can be transformed into a jewel of great beauty in your temple, even as deep suffering can bring divine revelation. So put away any sense of injury and look out upon the world with a calm love.

You are all more or less guilty of the tendency to worry, and to be consumed with anxiety and foreboding. If only we could show you the bogeys which this worry produces, what unhealthy, miserable spectres they are! You would not choose to keep such company!

My children, there is no need to fear *anything*; for even if that which you fear comes to pass, there is always a wise and loving power which bears you up and carries you safely over the rough places. Spiritual laws govern all life, God knows your every need. If difficult experiences come to you they come through the wisdom and love of your Father–Mother God. Why then be anxious about the future? Hold up your head, square your shoulders and accept your karma with thankfulness, knowing that it comes to help you. Think constructively, know that the future brings good and not evil. Refuse to attract bogeys! As the sun shining through the rain creates a rainbow, so also with each human life which looks to the sunlight of God. God will send nothing but good, and cares for your loved ones with a love infinitely greater than your own.

Be careful to send forth no thoughts of fear which might push others down the precipice of their own weakness, but rather by a constantly positive and constructive thought make yourself a rescuer. This is world service.

Thought is a matter of habit, and, as we have already said, human thought is mostly untidy and nebulous; but you who have set your feet upon the path must train your-selves in the habit of right thought, for the discipline of thought-control and thought-direction is absolutely necessary to those who would become conscious of the invisible worlds. Try at the outset to rule your thoughts for but one moment. Make a start by letting your mind dwell on some beautiful picture of the Master, or giving all the atten-tion of your heart and mind to a beautiful flower. Another symbol we like is that of a still candle-flame. Hold the thought, quiet and still, for as long as you are able, trying to extend the duration a little each time you perform the exercise.

Once you can control your thoughts you will begin to be of value to the Master and to your own guide as an instrument of the light. Your power will increase until your own light will shine forth to uplift, inspire and cheer those about you. Even those living on the astral plane will come closer for help and strength. It is so true, so true – *I, if I be lifted up from the earth* – I, the Christ within – *I will draw all men unto me.* And that truth applies to us all.

O God, we thank Thee for all Thy blessings, for the presence of the angels of light, for the understanding which comes to us; for the love which we feel for our brother, for the aspiration and the worship which we feel in our hearts. For all good thoughts, we thank Thee, O God. May we be strong in Thy love, Thy beauty and Thy truth.

Amen.

⊚

∾⊘

6

MORE ABOUT THE POWER OF THOUGHT

Let us pray in spirit to the source of our being, Father, Mother and the Son, holy and blessed Trinity. We thank Thee, O Great White Spirit, for all good, for all beauty, all truth. May we be ever conscious of Thy blessing, and of the outpouring of Thy love. We call in Thy name upon the angels of light. We pray that we may be receptive to their ministry to us. May there go forth from this group good thought, good will, and spiritual light. May we be servers of the light!

Amen.

BELOVED children, we greet you with love; we trust that your hearts will be stirred by the golden radiance now enfolding you. Truly the angels of light draw very close to those who humbly seek to serve the Great White Spirit; for all service, when selfless, when given freely and lovingly, is inspired

---

by the angels of light working through the human soul. It is important, in these days, for you to recognize the power of these angels, and their place in the great plan of God for the evolution of mankind. In many religious teachings references are made to the battle of life, and sometimes the soul of man is referred to as a battle-ground between forces of good and evil. You all know that when the conflict between good and evil, or conscience and the lower self, rages in you, you suffer. These forces are represented by angels of light on the one hand, and on the other, angels of darkness; and man should ever seek the inspiration of the angels of light.

You are all responsive to mental influences. When thoughts of doubt, depression, fear and anxiety creep upon you, you say that these are only natural and human: but the truth is that you are picking up such thoughts because you attract them. Man is like a magnet, he draws to himself angels of creative light, or angels of darkness and destruction. The angels of light come close to those who humbly and truly seek to serve the Great White Spirit.

The purpose of man's life is that he shall

grow towards consciousness of his own God-qualities; and the way to do this is for him continually to rise in thought towards the spheres of light, continually to open himself to the constructive forces and to the creative power of God. Through experience, and in the deep silence of meditation and contemplation, man grows towards God; by meditation on the qualities of the divine Father and Mother he grows in spiritual stature until he becomes at last the perfect son of God.

It is one thing to learn about scientific facts, or to study spiritual or occult truth; but until you have built into your soul body the light-atoms, the constructive God-atoms, you cannot serve life as you would like to serve. It is one thing to know with your mind and another to know with your inner self; and to know with your inner self implies spontaneous good thought and spontaneous good action; spontaneous giving forth of that light which is love, which is creative, which is quickening the very vibrations of your world and your physical body.

We often say that all things will work out eventually for your comfort and peace and happiness; but you must work as well as pray, and you must also daily partake of an inner communion. You know this; but the demands of modern life seem so urgent that you forget the grave importance and need for this inner communion, the breaking of the bread of life. This, together with loving service in the world, will build into your being particles of light, transmute the darkness, and overcome destructive forces which play around and within you. This is the secret of alchemy, the ancient wisdom which has always been waiting for men to find – the secret of the transmutation of the dark, dull, heavy metal of gross matter into the pure gold of spiritual substance.

Instruments are now being built to register the vibrations of thought, or soul vibrations; instruments which will be the means of demonstrating to humanity the reality of invisible forces. Most of you have, in your homes, a receiving set able to register the waves passing through the ether; when you press a switch you hear music or see pictures coming, perhaps, from the other end of the earth, and you accept this as an ordinary happening. You speak into a telephone, and your friend answers you from perhaps many hundreds of miles away, though you hear the voice as clearly as if it were in the very room in which you stand.

These inventions are overcoming space and demonstrating that the ether is full of waves of sound, waves of light. But there are other waves to which you are learning to respond. You are learning to be consciously receptive to thought-waves. You are discovering that you yourselves are receiving stations, and that by exercise of your mind and will you can tune in to whatever station you desire. You can attune yourselves to rays from the angelic kingdom of beauty and light, or you can attune yourselves to spheres of darkness, selfishness and greed – and, because these forces are destructive, to ultimate death.

Nevertheless we must recognize that the forces of good and evil both proceed from the life of God. Many people cannot accept the truth that good and evil are both within the power of God, for God is omnipotent, omniscient, omnipresent, and man lives within the very heart of God. Yet God has two aspects, and when these are understood and rightly viewed man can see the purpose of what is called evil. For evil is in truth the unevolved and undeveloped aspect of life, and is also the consuming, the destructive force, the fire which tries man's mettle, and absorbs and removes that which has become unwanted. Many people think that by attacking they will help to rid the world of evil, but we would say that the illumined soul refrains from attack, and instead radiates love and light, beauty and truth.

So, when you are called upon by your karma to go through an experience from which you shrink, if you can surrender wholly and tranquilly to the eternal light, to the pure sweet life of Christ the Son, and feel the warmth, strength and comfort of his all-enfolding love, you will find your problem will be solved, and you will be carried unscathed through your experience. But if you try to attack that which threatens to overwhelm you, you give it life.

Learn to live in the spirit, my children. Be strong in your inner self, and you will then naturally live a harmonious and beautiful outer life. People think that by turning their attention to spiritual matters they will get little accomplished on earth, but this is not true. By strengthening the spirit within you, by attuning yourself to the great calm of the Christ and the teachers and saints of all time, your powers of execution grow more perfect; but when you allow yourself to be engulfed in confusion and chaos you can accomplish nothing. So be tranquil and know the peace of God and the joy of life; thus you will be raising the vibrations of all life, and also of the earth itself.

We say again, thought is the most powerful agent. Everything originates from the mind of God. All form originates from the mind, from thought. We want to make quite clear that the same forces are used both in white and in black magic, but it is the motive of the operator which turns them to good or bad use. Always it is the thought of the operator which creates either the white magic or the dark magic. As your poet says, 'There's nothing either good or bad, but thinking makes it so'.

Good, or white magic, is performed with the knowledge and the assistance of angels of light. White magic is a ritual performed by a good man, a man of light working from his heart centre. He loves. He does not try to impose his own will; he seeks nothing for himself, but works selflessly for the good of the many. In the new age, many groups working with the white light will spring up

---

49

all over the earth. To work in such a group requires the spirit of selfless service and dedication, which allies the server with the forces of light. But when someone wants to work entirely for himself, to draw everything to himself, to impose his will, then he is allied with the negative forces. The White Brother has no thought of self; his one desire is, by love and light to bless and raise all men to a higher state. He gives, without reservation, from the depths of his being. This selfless giving distinguishes the white from the dark magic.

So, beloved children, we would leave you with this thought. Daily endeavour to direct good thought, kind thought into the world. It is so simple. The life of the true Christ man is a positive force which can affect all of mankind. In the degree that you give out good thought you attract to yourself forces of good, you reach to the light and the spiritual life, and so you are building the golden temple of the soul.

The building or development of the higher mental body through which the Christ within can and will operate depends upon your habitual thought. Think of yourself as descending like a babe to this earth, in order not only to develop in yourself the qualities of the Son of God, but in the process to help all people develop and look towards the great light for their happiness and their redemption – which means their escape from the darkness of lower matter, and their return to the freedom of the sun world, the Christ kingdom.

You look abroad and you see chaos in many countries. Fear stirs in your heart. You feel anxious. You must neither be anxious nor fearful. We do not see the coming of a great war again, or a major cataclysm, but we see this continuing battle in the hearts of men and women, together with a great uprising of desire for good, for light. Do not look with pessimism upon present world conditions; but work and work and work from your innermost being to broadcast the message of the Brotherhood of the Light. We do not mean by word. We mean by sending forth rays of light. Broadcast the message throughout the world that *there shall be light*, and that all people shall be raised up by the power of the light. This is a time of preparation for the coming into incarnation of many illumined souls who will work out in the open with ordinary people. It will be what you might describe as another coming of the lords of the sun, or agents of the solar logos embodied as men, to walk and talk once more with the peoples of the earth.

7

CLEAR VISION

O Great White Spirit, may the blindfold fall from the eyes of these Thy children that they may behold the company of great teachers and angelic beings all around them. May they have faith and confidence in the truth of the eternal life of spirit.

May the presence of the Christ spirit shining through the personality of the beloved Son bless each one in this sanctuary of the spirit.

For Thy blessing, O Lord, we humbly and simply thank Thee.

Amen.

BELOVED children, before we speak to you of the things of the mind and the physical life, we remind you again of the prayer. May our eyes be opened to the glory of the heavens. When we speak of the heavens, we are not speaking of things of an imaginary nature. We are speaking of reality, the only reality which man will ever find, the reality of life in

God, in spirit. This is why, at the beginning of our talk, we draw your attention and your vision to the glory of the heaven world.

We who come to you from the spirit can speak with authority because we live in the spirit, as all the disciples of the beloved Christ, the great teacher of all mankind, live; far removed from the noise and inharmony of the physical life. So we describe to you the golden world of spirit where all is harmony and beauty. This life in the heaven world is open to every soul on earth. No matter how lowly or ignorant, by its own aspiration and service to its fellow creatures the soul has access to that golden world of God. It is so important for you to understand this and to establish the ideal in your heart. Your earth life pulls you down; your body limits and imprisons you within the five senses. But we remind you that the five senses are only a part of the senses which man has at his disposal; other senses, which will reveal the heaven world to him, are, in this time and age, slowly developing in his soul.

In course of time the soul and the spirit will unite and become as one. Now the spirit is above the soul; but rightly the soul is the garment, the body of the spirit, and is built

---

from the next ether surrounding physical life. You have been told that in meditation you can extend these physical senses to the higher ethers. You can absorb the power of your own spirit so that it stimulates the soul senses, enabling them to pass through to the physical brain an awareness of higher or heavenly things. You see with the eyes of the spirit. You see with your spirit and what you see is reflected on to the physical brain. This must be so. The physical brain is the recipient or reflector of the senses of the spirit, when the spirit is sufficiently developed to impress upon it the finer vibrations of the heaven world.

We want you to understand that every sense has its spiritual counterpart. There is spiritual vision, spiritual taste, spiritual hearing, a spiritual sense of smell, and a spiritual sense of touch. Now all these senses, when they are fully developed, will bring a sixth sense into operation in humanity in the new age. It is not easy for us to put into words exactly what this sixth sense is, but we will explain it in this way: as you learn to disentangle yourself from the heaviness of the earthly life and the earthly body and the limitation of the earthly mind, you are able to rise, shall we say, in a weightless state, right above the earth plane, and reach the heaven world in full consciousness. This is the state of consciousness attained by the sainted ones, the Christed ones, through all the ages – a state of consciousness described not only in your own Christian scriptures but in all the scriptures of the world.

Some of you may remember the first instrument which enabled man to hear sound waves coming across the ether. Today there are instruments which not only convey the sound waves across the ether from distant places, but which will convey the sound waves in the most fine and delicate music to man. There are even finer and more exquisite sound waves, heavenly sound waves, which the human instrument will be able to register in course of time. Light waves, too, will be registered by man's own instrumentality – not a mechanical instrument, but the instrument of his own soul and brain. You see, into every living man and woman are built receiving centres which so far, in most men and women, remain unused.

Now, together with the exploration of space, there is also coming a breakthrough into man's consciousness of life and activity in finer spheres all around him. Even now there is evidence of this breakthrough on every hand. Some people seem to have a natural sixth sense or a natural inborn ability to see into the worlds of spirit, the inner worlds. You yourselves have experienced this in flashes, and you will experience it more and more as you learn the true values of life. By this we mean, as you learn to withdraw your attention from earthly things and enter the silence, the silence of God.

Every man and woman and child has the power within their own soul to receive impressions of beauty, impressions of heavenly things from higher planes. And not only impressions of heavenly things, but also impressions coming from other people, other states of life. We repeat: God has placed within man's own soul a wonderful receiving instrument.

We are always talking of meditation because we know that by true, deep meditation the soul touches truth, and at the same time learns to develop all the finer senses. We said a few moments ago that some people are born with these inner senses awakened. This is because the soul thus endowed has an opportunity which has come as a result of past thought and action. His or her karma has earned this opportunity. It may be that in a past life he or she learnt in one of the mystery schools.

We would remind you that pupils who were accepted in the mystery schools first learnt the rules, or the laws, governing physical life; and they came to understand that obedience to the laws of physical life is of fundamental importance to the candidate on the spiritual path. For instance, every pupil who entered the mystery school of the Brotherhood of the Light began his studies by disciplining and purifying the physical body. He learnt to eat pure food. He learnt never to inflict cruelty or suffering upon the animal kingdom. He learnt of the vitality and life in the air – *prana*, our Indian brethren call it – and how to breathe in the life-forces of the air. He learnt the cleansing property of the element of water, not only for the physical body but also for the psyche, and therefore the neophyte made a ritual of his daily ablution.

He learnt how to draw strength from the earth, and how to absorb consciously into his being the life-giving rays of the sun. In other words, he was taught how he could be purified, revivified, and sustained by his attunement to the elements. The ancient people grew their food with knowledge and understanding not only of the physical but of spiritual law. They did not stimulate the earth artificially, but grew their food under natural conditions and called down upon the earth the Great White Light, this wonderful element of the light which is love, to stimulate life in the earth, and feed and sustain their vegetation.

As man learnt to use all those elements, in his daily life, his physical body became purer, lighter, less weighed-down with the earth; thus enabling his spirit to come into fuller contact, through his physical body, with other beings, with the whole great brotherhood of life.

Each one of you has the gift of the spirit within your own being, and it is through this spirit that you will learn to overcome death. Man on his evolutionary path will learn that death is only a transition from one level of matter to a higher ether, and that within him is the power to build a bridge across which he can travel in full consciousness into those higher spheres and communicate with his loved ones, see the life they are living, and enjoy with them the beauties of the heavenly garden, taste the heavenly fruit and drink the heavenly wine and eat the heavenly bread of life.

We leave you with our blessing: *may peace remain with you always.*

Don't let the material and dark thoughts hold you down. Refuse to be bound. Cut clear from the bondage of Egypt – the physical consciousness – and rise in sweetness and love into the arms of God.

———

☙

8

RELINQUISHING THE LOWER SELF

Let us arise and ascend the mountain, and from the higher planes of consciousness witness with clearness of vision the love streaming forth upon humanity. We see the wisdom guiding all life upward towards the light. O Great Spirit, eternal wisdom, may we dwell in Thy life, and may Thy life dwell in us!

Amen.

WE HAVE spoken to you on a number of occasions about the white magic, and of how the secret of all the mystery schools was the knowledge of how to use this magical power which lies dormant in all people. So-called miracles are demonstrations of this white magic; although we must add that no initiate will waste time and power to satisfy the curious. Demonstrations of this magic are only given to bless, to uphold, and to help souls to realize their divine potentialities.

In the mystery schools of old it was taught that no soul could rush forward into the temple. Indeed, the very nature of the spiritual unfoldment necessary before the soul can enter into the holy temple makes this impossible. Sometimes it seems a very long journey up the mountain, and souls get weary and discouraged and think that they will never reach their goal. We understand the weariness of the flesh and the mind and the spirit, but we know also that without fail a sustaining, refreshing grace comes, which upholds the weary traveller on his journey.

Knowledge purely as a mental attainment is of little use to the soul as it seeks entrance into the mysteries. This is why we encourage you to devote time to meditation and contemplation.

Now some think that meditation means to sit still thinking beautiful thoughts, but that in itself will not get you very far. Correct meditation releases the soul from the bondage of the physical senses and enables it to rise through the various planes of life right up to the peak at which illumination comes; and when illumination comes it brings with it knowledge. The soul practised in meditation learns to approach the temples of wisdom, and there, in the silence, receives from the teachers the knowledge and the understanding of spiritual law which it seeks. Some are able to rise only to a limited height; they see writing, they see symbols, or characters in a language they do not understand. The symbols, the characters mean nothing until the soul has the key which will enable it to interpret the symbols.

Now, the pupil in the mystery schools is taught that the key to understanding of these symbols is in the golden chamber; and the golden chamber is the heart, called by some the golden lotus; and within this golden flower lies the key which will unlock the door of the mysteries. You can read many books. You can accumulate many facts. You can go through ceremonies. You can witness or even take part in wonderful rituals which will stir your emotional body, or even stimulate the higher mind to a degree – but none of these will of themselves give you the power to enter the temple and understand the secrets of the inner mysteries.

Everything needed by the aspirant for his entry into the Great White Lodge lies within himself. No school on the outer plane can give you this knowledge. The only school in which you will obtain this precious wisdom is in the school of life; you will learn through human life and experience and human relationships on the outer plane, and through meditation on the inner plane. The outer action and the inward contemplation and meditation must go hand in hand if the aspirant is seeking the lost secret, the divine magic.

In the mystery schools every candidate is led eventually to a chapel or a cell which has no furnishings but a mirror, and he has to be ready and strong enough to look into the mirror and see the true reflection of himself. A soul has so many thick and dark coverings of human weakness and self-deception, and all these have to be shed until the soul stands quite naked before its reflection. To the one who is truly searching this can be a moment of divine illumination. It is a moment of initiation when everything extraneous is shed, and the soul rises and becomes united with the source of its being.

Now, you may begin to see why meditation and outward living must go hand in hand, because in meditation the soul becomes aware of truth, and the life lived must be a demonstration of the truth revealed in meditation.

Heaven is a state of supreme happiness and joy, reached when the soul comprehends the power of the divine magic. Yet this magic is so elusive, and cannot be put into words; it is a divine essence with which the soul is filled, almost unconsciously. A master is natural, is all love, is gentle. A master dominates no-one but loves all. Thus does he demonstrate the divine magic, and the divine magic is a power which will remove every obstacle, overcome all difficulties, make crooked places straight. It will bring peace in place of storm. The Master Jesus demonstrated this, when he rose in the boat and stilled the waves. The boat is a symbol of the soul. His very presence – the divine presence, the divine magic – overcame the storm of emotion.

Do you see the reason why karma is a barrier? Karma, my children, is really unlearned lessons. These lessons have to be faced in a calm spirit. Rejoice in your karma. Thank God for the opportunities which are presented to you to learn lessons and dispose of your karma, for these are steps by which

---

you mount into the Great White Lodge above. Every piece of karma gone through means a lesson learned, but the most important thing for you to remember is do not just try to get past your karma; be sure you have learned the lesson which the episode was intended to teach. If you have not learnt the lesson and have just skirted around your karma, you have only put it on the shelf and it will come back again and again until the lesson has been learned.

Is this hard? But it is true, and we are trying to show you and to help you, because we love you. We are your brethren. We have passed your way. We have ways to travel beyond and beyond and beyond the earth, but when we look upon karma, the obstacle-lessons which are placed before us, we accept them with thanksgiving. This is why we say, on many occasions: accept, accept, accept the conditions in your life and be thankful for them, for they are steps leading to illumination and perfect happiness.

The secret of the divine magic comes to you when you have overcome, when you have learnt to master the lower self and to manifest divine love, gentleness, kindness: when you have learnt not to retaliate or be resentful. The initiate resigns all injustice, however great or small, to divine law. He knows that the oil-press of the law crushes the olives, and the oil of wisdom remains. The hardships, the inequalities, the difficulties, the injustices of life are all ground in the press of God, and the pure oil of wisdom, the pure wine of life, remains.

The wise man or woman will not seek to justify himself or herself, but resigns all in perfect confidence and faith to the exact outworking of the law of God, of love.

Now peace, true lasting peace, be with you. Remember the gentle way, the gentle answer, the relinquishing of all demands. Thy will, not my will, be done, O God.

Children, the Master is present. Open your hearts and receive His blessing. He stands in your midst, the perfect Son of God.

We bow before Him.

———

☺☺

9

LEARNING TO USE THE INNER SENSES

God our Father, in whom we live and move and have our being, we would become aware of Thy love and wisdom. We would open our eyes that we may walk forward into the light, and our ears that we may hear the voice of the spirit, and be channels for the power and radiance of Thy truth. May Thy light dispel the darkness of earth, and may Thy love bring peace into the hearts of men. May the spirit of peace and tranquillity and calm reign supreme in our hearts this night.

Amen.

WE WOULD bring more than love tonight: we would bring wisdom and the power which will fill your being with confidence and the realization of the invisible hosts of the light now ministering to humanity. Remember that however weak and insignificant you feel

ou can be a channel through
st light can manifest. You
ght to the very condition in
find yourself in order that
d to serve – you would not be
ords were it not so. You are a
rld, and must stand firm and
you know is truth – that the
ght of Christ is the healer of
and of soul. It can heal the
it can dispel the darkness of
It is the builder of all good,
cial time you are called by the
isible into service, into action.
serve?' we hear you ask. You
ur to become aware of the
s playing upon the earth life.
n your body and your higher
ome consciously aware of this
ht which finds entrance into
ough the psychic centres; you
become aware of this circulat-
am which vivifies and can
and soul, and pass from you,
directed by your highest self, to heal the sick
in body and mind throughout the world.
The angels and spiritual beings work
through human channels to build heaven

into the consciousness of man. This is ancient wisdom. In the temple training of the past, men and women were taught to become aware of the world of light within the soul.

In Egypt, colour rays were used to heal both body and soul. The wise teacher in that age taught his pupil to attune himself to the first great cause – the sun; to become in harmony with the sun and with the light; to develop that attitude of mind which could neither think nor do harm to any living thing. Thus the pupil made himself a channel; he absorbed the light of the sun through every centre, or chakra, in the body, reaching through the chakras to the higher bodies: through the seven chakras to the seven vehicles of man.

At the head of the seven rays of life within which all creatures have their being, are the great masters of wisdom, and beyond them the archangels – shall we call them the angels round the throne? Radiating throughout life from the centre, from the heart, we find these seven rays, and from each one another seven, and from each again another seven, until behind the veil of physical life are unveiled countless beings, both of the human line of evolution, and of nature; and we see the life of every growing thing brought into manifestation and sustained by the harmonizing work of these countless hosts.

Let us visualize the sun, the centre of your solar system, the spiritual sun invisible behind the sun, and the spiritual rays descending upon humanity, blending, harmonizing, weaving a glorious rainbow of colour and beauty throughout creation, working in the most beautiful and wonderful way to convey to the consciousness of man the divine glory of his true being. Ultimately the colour and beauty resolves itself back again into that perfect light, the great white light. There is no such thing as chance, no such thing as accident: everything works by perfect law, under the direction of the great beings at the head of these rays which permeate humanity.

In the mystery schools of the past, the pupil was taught about the effect of colour upon the soul, upon the mind, upon the body, the effect of perfume, the effect of sound. Colour, perfume and sound. It is a pity that so few today realize how powerfully these three affect human life.

———

Some respond more to vibrations of sound, some to perfume, some to colour. Some will be influenced deeply, if sometimes unconsciously, by colour in their surroundings; while for others the harmony of music, sound, will cause their souls to open to the sunlight, to the white light of the sun, of the Christ. To others the angels or the dwellers in the land of light will convey their message by the fragrance of perfume, through the sense of smell. Certain masters, particularly, use the vibration of perfume to impress their presence upon a pupil. Sometimes you may smell incense, or perhaps the perfume of a rose, and you say, 'O what lovely perfume, I wonder where it comes from!' Actually you have received a ray, a thought, from a wise one, and this is your particular way of reacting. Not your conscious mind, but your soul, reacts to that subtle stimulation towards higher things. It may happen that a discarnate spirit, one you have loved, will bring to you a perfume which brings a memory, an association, perhaps of a hayfield, roses, violets, or the beautiful earth wet with the gentle rain, or perhaps the scent of pines — these arouse in you a memory, and that memory will link you with your beloved.

———

Some wonder why we do not disapprove of flowers being taken away from the parent root. Because the flowers bring themselves as gifts to humanity. The little nature spirits who work with the flowers come as messengers into our homes, into our sanctuaries, sending forth the vibrations of harmony and colour and perfume to reach the hearts and touch the souls of humankind. We would go so far as to say that some of you at a service may have received more from the vibrations of the flowers upon the altar than from any word which has been spoken. The flowers speak, and their vibrations or those of the little nature spirits working with them can convey to your soul the message God would have you receive.

In meditation you are learning to develop the senses of your soul, so that you become aware, through these senses, of the inner life of the soul. Through your higher senses, so will you become more attuned, more awakened, more aware of the eternal life of the spirit.

Concerning the rays of colour we are learning to use for healing, we would not bind you to any dogmatic teaching. In the spiritual life we see a gentle blending and

---

harmonizing of all colour, and it is difficult to separate one from another. Yet we do see them as separate, each with its individual influence and effect. Can you understand? To say that a specific colour can always be used for the same purpose is not correct. According to the receptivity or development of the soul of the patient, so will the colour vary. According to the need or the vibration, so the colour changes. Thus we have blues from the very palest to the very deepest, subtly blending according to the need and receptivity of the patient. Can we say that each of those colours has seven aspects each broken up again into seven, seven, seven, seven . . . each producing a different blending of colour? All these subtle colour vibrations have their particular work to do upon the seven vehicles of man.

So also with music, and the seven notes of the diatonic scale in different combination create by their vibration the seven colour rays, which you could see if your eyes were open. Look, next time you listen to music, and imagine the colours which certain themes produce. Where music has been performed a great deal, a vibration has been originated and is going forth all the time.

Music lingers long after the sound has died away. Therefore music performed in this Lodge helps to create the vibration which we love so much – healing, stimulating, health-giving, to the soul coming into the Lodge.

Certain modern music appears to have a disintegrating effect, but bear in mind that sounds of that kind have their special work to do in breaking down certain mental conditions, certain forms. Remember, there must be a clearing away as well as a building. This is a fact to bear in mind with life generally. Learn to see good, even in destruction, recognizing it as a cleansing process in preparation for the next step. Often there must be disintegration before there can be re-creation.

Music originates in the creative spheres of art, and is directed through the higher mind of the composer. Although he does not realize it, the composer receives inspiration from great angels responsible for creation of beauty in form, and the spiritual life in men on earth.

One of the most wonderful revelations the soul experiences after it has left earthly conditions and awakens in its true home in the heaven world, is the beauty of colour.

———

You all love a garden of flowers; you look upon the flowers and wonder at their colour and form. The colours which you see are as nothing compared with the flowers in the invisible worlds, and indeed, there are colours in heaven of which you have no knowledge.

Such colouring results from the spiritual harmony of the beholder. One who sees the beauty of the heavenly colours does so because he or she has become at one with that white light of God, the focal point of all light, and within that white light is the Trinity, the basis of all life.

You can carry about with you your world of colour. You are clothed in colour. Your thoughts and emotions create the colours which you wear. Joseph's brothers tried to rob him of his coat of many colours, but a man or woman cannot rob another of this many-coloured coat. Each is clothed in his particular coat, the colours resulting from thoughts and speech, emotions and aspirations, and ranging from crude, violent shades up to the fine celestial shades which indicate the celestial body; or which, to be correct, form the celestial body and thus clothe the spirit of the true child of God.

———

This clothing has also its own perfume. Each colour has a distinct perfume. The masters and elder brethren can register the perfume of the aura with great accuracy and from a distance. Also the aura contains sound. The aura can give forth beautiful harmonies, or it can emit vibrations like a piece of violent music – or perhaps the word noise would be better.

Imagine, if you can, the gathering together of a large company of men and women in the heaven world, each soul contributing its quota of harmony, of sound, and perhaps you will conceive something of the music which a company of radiant souls can create. Strive to live a little closer to these heavenly realities and you will find that this awareness will not incapacitate you from doing your work on earth. On the contrary, as you draw closer to God and to the harmonies of the heavenly places, so your ability to serve the needs of your fellows in a practical manner will increase.

———

☙

10

THE PATH OF MEDITATION IS ONE OF SERVICE

Dear brethren, we come into your midst praying that each may absorb the light; that the aura of the whole gathering may be purified, so that it can receive the rays of life, of truth, and not only hear the words, but hear in the heart the message.

Amen.

IT IS so difficult for you, whilst living on a plane limited by time and space, to understand what we mean when we say there is no time; but when you can rise above the level of the earthly mind and go, in meditation or in spirit, to the plane of the Christ consciousness, you can for a flash realize your unity with the whole of life and comprehend the meaning of the eternal 'now'. You then touch what you understand as cosmic consciousness.

This should be the whole object of your meditations – love for and union with God, source of your being. You desire nothing for yourself, nothing which will enhance your own powers, or glorify yourself. You have but one thought, one object, which is adoration of the Beloved, a seeking to draw closer, to merge into and become part of the Beloved. What is the Beloved? The Beloved is God, is universal life in all its manifestations. In your meditation you become consciously at one with universal life. It is, as your Eastern teachers tell you, the act of the dewdrop merging into the ocean.

To some Western minds the idea of such a unification is distasteful, for Western man clings to the idea of individualization, and of development of his or her own personality. But when the soul becomes filled with love for its Creator it no longer seeks its own advancement; on the contrary, selflessness, gentleness, self-abnegation – these are the soul qualities of the one who has truly set his feet on the path of meditation – qualities which you recognize in the Lord Jesus, or the Lord Krishna, the Lord Buddha, and all the great world teachers.

The path of meditation is one of selfless

devotion to the One Being, God, the Perfect One. Do not seek for either psychic power or psychic unfoldment on the path of meditation. These powers may come, but psychic power is wisely withheld in some incarnations because the soul's karma may make it dangerous for that soul to develop psychically before the coming of spiritual illumination. Instead of a search for psychic power, let your object be simple devotion to the Great White Spirit, to the Beloved.

You know that you have certain centres of nerve-force in your body which we call the 'chakras'. You know also that in most people these centres of nerve-force are unawakened and dull, but that they can be vivified by certain procedures. In the method of meditation which we unfold, we are imparting a way by which you yourself can awaken the true spiritual life which is within you. A healer can help a patient, a teacher can teach a pupil, but the patient or the pupil must also work for himself. Meditation is a path which must be faithfully pursued, for it may take years, a whole lifetime in the body, or indeed a number of lifetimes, for the pupil to reach the splendid goal. You cannot hurry this process. It is necessary to keep on keeping on patiently, but much time can be wasted when you are not conversant with the true purpose for which you work, which is, in truth, a conscious union with the God from whom you come.

This constant awareness of the soul's true source, the constant awareness of its relationship to God, is very important. The man who loves, and who is aware of God's all-enfolding love manifesting everywhere, even if he has no set form of meditation: such a one naturally reaches the goal of conscious union with God, with universal Spirit.

Realization such as this may come occasionally and in flashes and sometimes without being sought. For others it will seem a goal very far in the distance. But if you remain pure in aspiration, and loving to your fellow creatures, you may at any time in your life be blessed with illumination resulting from conscious union between you, the individual, and universal Spirit. Whether you know it or not, whether you believe it or not, during this life *all souls* are travelling towards this union with God; and as you progress, both through meditation and by continually practising love in your life, by giving kindness and service to all creatures, you will be developing a spiritual life within you which will enable you to master the events of your daily life, to become master of yourself at every level of your being.

Now when you meditate you rise to a much higher plane than that at which you normally function, and at that level you find yourself outside the bounds of time, so that memories of past experience may become alive for you. At that level of consciousness also you can touch the heart of truth; the evolution of your life is made clear to you and you know that past, present and future are all one. You know eternity.

To reach that point of consciousness requires long practice and perseverance, devotion to God, devotion to your work, devotion to human needs, service to humanity. Meditation will carry you a long way, but with meditation you must also have the life of service and kindness, peace and tranquillity. Then you cannot help but pierce the mists of earth and find truth.

Once you recognize yourself as *spirit*, development and growth towards full awareness at every level of consciousness begins. The words, *Eye hath not seen, nor ear heard . . . the things which God hath prepared for them that love him,* are indeed true. Your limited consciousness cannot comprehend these glories; nor can you realize the vast unseen life which is all around you. But meditation will help you towards this inner vision and realization. And remember always the loving wisdom of God and of those elder brethren who have traversed the same path as every soul must tread. They understand, and they come to help you on the path which leads to spiritual realization and illumination, and union with God.

෧෧

11

CHANGING THE BASE METAL INTO GOLD

We raise our consciousness to the Most High, to the Infinite Spirit, our Father–Mother God. May we be strengthened in the light of His Son, Christ, the perfect man of earth and heaven. May His beauty inspire our lives and work; His wisdom direct our lives and work; and his Love make manifest His work in us, through us, to all living things.

Amen.

WE HAVE spoken about the life of the aspirant. The object and the goal of the mystic has been the same throughout all ages; advanced brethren of every race have become pioneers and teachers for the rest to follow. You have no doubt read of alchemists in the middle ages who sought the philosophers' stone, or the means of transmuting base metal into gold. The Brethren of the Rose Cross are said to have had this secret.

Certainly it is true that in the process of spiritual development the soul gains knowledge of the constitution of matter and its relationship to spiritual qualities and powers. To the master, the production of gold is simple, but no master would waste his knowledge in producing gold for greedy people, and certainly not for himself. He would have no use for it; but if it served some good purpose, he could easily produce gold for the needs of the community. However this changing of base metal into gold is really a symbol, which hides the deeper truth of the transmutation of the nature of man from the worldly to the spiritual.

Now the whole purpose of life is this gradual transmutation of the physical senses, of the material person, into the saint, the spiritual being. That is, the transmutation of the lead of the lower nature into the pure gold of the highest, spiritual self. And the only path we know to this goal is that of true meditation. In your busy Western world you have a difficult task, because the West concentrates upon action. Eastern thought, the Eastern way of life, is more contemplative and quiescent. In the Western world the pull of matter is so strong that you find it difficult to set aside time, even in your own home, to meditate. But you will be so richly rewarded, my children, if you earnestly and devotedly give time each day to meditation. You will also find it a great help to meditate with a group. Some find it more difficult to meditate alone because of the many distractions, not necessarily on the physical but on the astral and mental planes. Using a mantra, a word of power, helps to break down such distractions. The power of sound, of the word, rightly spoken, penetrates and dissolves all unwanted thought-forms and intrusive thoughts, thus purifying the mental atmosphere.

You are told to use your power of visualization, to create in your mind's eye a picture, a form. This is to centralize your aspiration, and help to still the busy mind of earth, the lower mind. Visualization, coupled with devotion and aspiration, will bring the true communion between yourself and God. When you meditate, try to focus your whole attention on the manifestation of God in form; try to 'imagine' or create for yourselves the form of the Perfect One, the highest that you can conceive. Feel the love and strength which emanates from this beautiful figure. Your own highest self will manifest in the Perfect One that you have conceived. It is difficult to put into words a state of consciousness which cannot be described, an experience which takes place in the heart.

In the degree that you feel love for your fellow creatures, in the degree that you feel love for life, you will find your aura and your heart centre expanding to encompass all life. When all thought of self dies you will realize the divine ecstasy, the goal of mystics and saints of all time; and the joy which the aspirant experiences in true meditation is beyond anything which the worldly man can understand or gain from earthly success and pleasure.

We would make absolutely clear the fact that you will not realize your goal through mental pursuit, through your mind, but only in the innermost sanctuary of your spirit, of your heart; and when you have reached that, you will find expansion of consciousness so that you become aware of all spheres of life. You will realize your at-one-ment with the eternal Spirit, and past, present and future

---

will be one to you, for you will be living in eternity. You will comprehend the mysteries of the universe. You will recognize, while still living in the body, the difference between your true self and this bodily shell. You will have attained freedom of action, because even though karma will continue to beset you during the physical life, you will at the same time have learned the secret of transmuting your karma. You will use the difficulties of your karma to lead you into greater and more beautiful service.

Do not forget the importance of rhythmic and deep breathing, because as you breathe deeply and from your heart centre you are affecting not only the physical, but also all the subtler bodies, in particular the mental and the astral bodies. The mind and the emotions can both be stilled by quiet, slow and gentle breathing, but realize that it is the breath of the divine life which you breathe. Sit with your spine straight (because the forces travel up the centre of the body) and then, breathing slowly and deeply, consciously breathe in the light and vital life. Then gently release the breath, thinking of it as light, a light which can reach all life. The whole object is to bless and to uplift all forms of life. If you feel this divine fire in your heart it will come as strength. If when you are tired you practise your yogic breathing, you will find yourself charged with vitality, and will not know weariness. The soul who attains union with the source of all being attains mastery over himself, over life, and over age. When you understand how to remain attuned to the source of all life, the physical body is renewed. *They that wait upon the Lord shall renew their strength.*

You have heard us say before that the human body can be likened to a temple. Within this temple is an altar on which burns a bright clear flame. In your meditation seek this altar; try to imagine it, and bow your head in surrender before that altar flame within your temple. You yourself are creating this glowing altar and the light upon it. It is real, for it is being generated by you, is arising in you; and thus you see it in the form of an altar blazing with light. This is not your imagination; it is what you are actually creating by your aspiration, by your will, by concentration and direction of your thought. The flame which you see upon the altar may take the form of a rose with a brilliant jewel of light shining at its centre. If you see this in your meditation, remember that you are gazing upon your own heart centre. Or it may take the form of a pure white lotus with its many petals – again your own unfolding inner self. The chakras instead of being closed and dull are opening like flowers in the sunlight because of your meditation and aspiration.

Thus, through aspiration and the will of God within, you create in meditation your inner world, your temple. By soul effort the aspirant is building the very temple that he beholds. It is created, by an effort of will, out of the seer's soul substance and the light within. Astral atoms are as real as physical atoms, but are without form until moulded by the will of the aspirant. Realize that in your meditation you are working with the substance of God, which is eternal; and that within the centre of your own being God has given you the power to create form. In your meditation you are using this power to create and mould form at the inner level, on the astral and etheric plane; but the time will come when you can use this creative power at the physical level. When an evolved soul achieves mastery over the physical life by the power of spiritual will, it also achieves mastery over the atoms of the physical body. These atoms gradually become purified, or, as we say, 'transmuted', so that they shed the darker substance of the earth. In the same way, the body in which you will find yourself when your present form is shed will be of a much finer substance but the same in appearance as your physical body. As the soul grows, gradually the heavier atoms fall away and the soul becomes etherealized, ever growing more beautiful as it mounts towards the celestial kingdom where all life is pure and perfect.

As you become practised in meditation you will feel tremendous power on occasion. Unless this power becomes purified by devotion, love and aspiration it may tend to overwhelm you. Try, however, calmly to direct it outward into the world, thinking with compassion of all who suffer. Send out the light to them. This is the way of the initiates of all ages. All are directing this same light out into the world. It is only because of this light continually sent forth from these enlightened and advanced souls in the world of light that human life continues. Without it, war and cataclysm would have overwhelmed mankind. You may not have thought of this, nor realized that within yourself, as in every man and woman, as well as the creative power of good, is a strong pull towards earthliness, towards darkness. But the object of man's life is that he shall find liberation from earthliness, shall find mastery over matter. Man has to rise in the full glory of the Lord, and so God has endowed him with qualities which when developed will liberate him from all suffering, and in the end from death itself.

12

THE WAY TO THE INNER MYSTERIES

We humbly invoke the blessing of the Most High, holy and blessed Trinity, the source of all being. We pray, O Father–Mother–Son, that Thy spirit may be in our hearts; and that being raised in consciousness to the source of light and truth we may hold true communion of spirit with spirit and with the angels; that we may feel our at-one-ment with all life on earth and in heaven. May wisdom and understanding bless each soul.

Amen.

MANY SEEK to be let into secrets. They seek the mysterious, the occult truth beyond the sight and knowledge of ordinary people. They seek by joining secret societies or by much reading, or other intellectal pursuits. But the key to all knowledge is found only through attunement to the divine Spirit. It is the spirit within which holds the secret of all

———

wisdom, and until that spirit is touched and unfolds through the soul's own aspiration and will, the mysteries remain closed and secret; they remain secret until the spirit quickens and the soul rises into the halls of wisdom, to the place of divine illumination.

In fact there are no secrets, because all knowledge is within you. But that inner knowledge, that inner power, must remain covered and secret until the soul has attained to a degree of understanding of spiritual law so that it can use this developed power wisely. In the mystery schools, the method of development was imparted by slow degrees to those who were ready, and the candidate was helped to rise in consciousness through the guidance and love of the brothers in those schools.

Imagine how you would feel if you were able to go, now, into a temple of wisdom in the inner world and receive instruction in these secrets. Having been conducted to the hall of wisdom and learning you could choose to study music, art, literature, science, healing, religion, ancient civilizations, astronomy, astrology – all this knowledge would be opened to you. To a degree this can happen whilst you are on earth, although on earth there always appears to be a mist obscuring the greater glory. In our teaching we are endeavouring to touch not your minds, but your hearts, so that wisdom and understanding may unfold to your heart mind; and so that your hearts may become aware of the all-enfolding love and beauty of the spirit life. We are trying to help you to realize that the spirit life interpenetrates the physical — that there is no 'here' and 'over there' in the way you think, but that all is one eternal life. There is no barrier between matter and spirit, but an interpenetration of the two. You are clothed in a dense garment and yet at the same time you live in a world of light, companioned, if you so will, by beings of great beauty and wisdom, beings beautiful not only in appearance but in character, because they have unfolded that inner knowledge and wisdom into full consciousness.

The contact with those in the world of light is not made through the brain, nor through the solar plexus, but in the heart. Through the solar plexus the planes of feeling and emotion and desire are contacted; from the throat and the frontal centre of the head, the mental plane; but from the

———

heart you reach beyond all these and go right to the centre of all truth. This is why mystics were often humble, hard-working men and women. They had neither time nor opportunity for great mental achievement, but they loved their Creator, loved all things beautiful and gentle, they loved all life and through that love drew close to God: to the supreme spirit, Christ, the Son. Then divine wisdom was theirs.

The surest way to the heart of the mysteries is to cultivate love, is to emulate the spirit of Jesus the Christ. If you will meditate on love, and on the loving presence of the Master, you will absorb the golden light of the Christ being into your heart, and gradually you will be changed. You will know what it means to be happy; what it means to be at peace.

From the beginning of life when the Christ spirit baptized the earth, brought life into being on this earth, this inner knowledge has always been with man, but it has been hidden, covered by many layers of earthiness. The ancient wisdom which is the foundation of all religions was brought to mankind in the beginning of the cycle by those whom we will call God-men or Sun-men, brothers of the light who came to earth from afar bringing their wisdom to a young humanity, pure in spirit; teaching them the law of God and a way of life which would lead them through the bondage of physical matter back again to God, as fully God-conscious beings, themselves men and women of God.

Ever since the earth was peopled it has passed through ages of varying consciousness. Golden ages have come and gone as a new and young race was born and gradually grew to Christ-manhood. The human race is not very evolved today, but it will become great again when the secret power within mankind has been released and the whole vibration of the earth thereby raised. Man contains within himself the secret of good and evil. At present it would seem that mankind is responding more to the pull of the evil or the negative aspect, and there has to come a stimulation of this light and love in his heart. When this happens he will recover from selfishness and overcome the downward pull, and then the whole earth will change.

The beings we have described are of rare beauty and they are still with you, though not in physical form. When you meditate you dimly feel their influence, and as you persevere in your meditations you will become increasingly aware of them. These brethren, who are masters of your life, watch over you and your spiritual good. They love you; they will always come if you sound the correct password.

Now you will say, 'Tell us the password, White Eagle'. This is one of the teachings of the ancient mystery schools. More important than any vocal sound is the word spoken in the heart. It is in the heart that the true password is sounded. You cannot slip into the halls of wisdom unless you clearly sound that password — and it is the vibration of pure brotherhood. It is a soul vibration of the absolute brotherhood of life. It is not easy; but you see, my children, you are learning to sound the password in your ordinary human contacts — in your home, in your office, in your daily service; wherever you are, whatever your duty, you are being given opportunity to learn the password. In other words, if you are living rightly you are attuning yourself to the infinite love and wisdom and are bringing it right through into everyday life with every word and action.

You can be sounding the password even when you do the most menial task; and when you think of the need of your companion kindly and conscientiously, not pushing past, or closing your ear to the urge which says, Do this; it is kind, it is helpful. Be thoughtful for this woman, who is tired and weary. Be kind to that man, who has had great sorrow. To learn the password means to be on the alert always to the spirit of the Son of God. When you can do this by action and thought, you initiate a vibration in your soul which sounds throughout the spheres of spiritual life. It is a challenge, a command, a vibration which goes from you which the Master receives without fail and which immediately attunes you to him. You are at one with him, and then there comes an ever-increasing flow of this inner, this secret magic. Then understanding expands and power comes to perform what earthly people call miracles.

These things were taught in all the ancient mystery schools. They are taught today. Beings from those ancient days are coming back in greater power to help man to find the secret spring of life within. It will depend upon him whether he will receive. He can receive – *when* he wills. But we tell you that the world has arrived at a critical stage – you all know this. Spiritual knowledge must – and will – flood the earth to preserve its equilibrium. You have been called to the service of the light.

13

THE TRANSFORMING POWER

Beloved bretheren, you are raised in spirit into the golden world of God, where all thoughts of the physical and material life leave you, for you are opening your hearts now to the eternal spirit of love. . .

May the light of the Christ, shining through the personality of the beloved Son, bless and fill you with joy and thankfulness.

Amen.

WE WOULD speak to you about the transforming power which is within all children of God, the divine light which can transform their earthliness and make them true sons and daughters of God. We often speak to you about this sun, about the light within your hearts. You will grow weary maybe of the repetition of this one truth; but, my brethren, it is the only truth in life. Upon this foundation the whole structure of mortal and spiritual life is built. It is therefore vitally important that you comprehend more and more of the light of God in yourselves, and above all as it manifests in His supreme Son, Christ, Lord of the earth planet. How can you best realize more of this light within yourselves in your daily life? Quite simply, by putting into effect the words of Jesus – *love one another*. Those three words, if truly understood and lived, would set the whole world aflame with power, with happiness and with plenty.

What happens when the soul simply and wholly lives to love and serve its fellow creatures? That soul is strengthening the link between its spirit and the Great White Spirit, all glorious, all powerful, almighty, the blazing sun of light. By love, contact between the soul and God is confirmed, and light pours into the soul. Then it is building the body of light which is the wedding garment spoken of in the parable. No soul, even though it passes from the physical, can enter into the heavenly life unless it is thus clothed in light.

Through all religions you will find instruction in how to bring into operation this light of the spirit which lies dormant in every man. The whole purpose of life in the flesh is to develop this power, through love; not through any mental pursuit, which is the mistake many are making in this mental age of Aquarius. This is why groups such as this one have a big part to play at this time. Many people read book after book after book, and their brains are filled with reading matter. But something more is needed – the wisdom of the heart, and love; because love is the light. Your mental body may be very strong; but unless your heart is filled with love and with loving service you cannot use the know-ledge which you have acquired. You cannot even control it; it will control you. It will absorb you. This is why the development of the simple light of love in the heart is so important at the present time, because with-out it the immense power of this mental age is likely to absorb and destroy men. Don't be fearful about this, for we are telling you of the counteracting influence. We only emphasize the danger of this mental stim-ulation without a corresponding goodness of heart and loveliness of character.

Within you all lies opportunity to grow in spirit, to grow in stature until you become as the Master, for did he not tell you, *The works that I do shall ye do also?* Hold the ideal ever before you. Be strong in spirit, do not be cast down. It is good to recognize shortcomings, for humility is a true companion of the aspirant on the path; keep your feet on the earth, yes, but lift your face towards the heavens, for the light which floods into you from on high will steady your feet and guide them in the right path. Have confidence in this divine light. Surrender to it with a tranquil mind and a heart full of love for God. We are not speaking of some nebulous and incomprehensible force, far distant from you. This divine fire is within your very being, and as you raise your face and open your heart to the sun, the rays of the sun stimulate the divine light within you. Work to bring this light into manifestation in you, not in haste but quietly, gently, with mind and heart fixed steadily upon God.

Seek and ye shall find. The Master did not speak idly. The soul which seeks always finds. Sometimes the answer is found instantly; sometimes a whole life may be lived before the answer comes, but come it will, for there is always an answer to the search of the soul.

———

Sometimes, in sleep, your guide will take you to the halls of wisdom where you receive an answer in your innermost consciousness to the questions of your heart. But the spirit has powers of contact with the Most High, with the Creator, the great sun, beyond that of the soul. There is no time or space in the realms of spirit. Instantly the spirit within man can make its contact. Unfortunately this contact is usually only just enough to keep life flowing into the physical body. Later, as the soul evolves, it grows to yearn more and more for the divine light, and calls and prays for knowledge. Then teachers come from spheres of light to that soul, or they may make use of an even more evolved soul on earth to convey instruction to the younger brother. Souls learn the wisdom of God through countless incarnations. The soul needs long contact with physical matter to enable it to use the creative power of the light, implanted deep, deep within.

But every two thousand years the earth receives anew a baptism of the Christ light, the spiritual sunlight. When this occurs the sons of God, the illumined ones, the great ones, are sent to help humanity. Messengers are coming even now to quicken the vibrations and to raise fallen humanity to their feet so that they will stand upright ready to welcome and recognize their Lord when he returns. Many people are asking: Is Christ coming again in the form he wore before? Or will he secretly enter the hearts of the people? We say: in both ways. The light has first to be quickened in the people so that they will recognize the divine Son when he comes. *Watch and pray*, said Jesus, *for you know not the day nor the hour when the Son of Man cometh*. Be ready; work; love.

Put on the garment of light. Live the life of love and service. Live in the spirit. Live in the conscious contact with the spiritual realms and you will not neglect the physical plane, but on the contrary will execute your duties with greater thoroughness, with more precision and perfect order. The brethren who have passed on before you work with you for this coming of the Christ; but not only must you work in service and in love amongst your fellows, but within your soul you must learn to meditate and hold communion with the source of your being; for the time is near when every man will be his own priest and every woman her own priestess, and receive, kneeling before the altar within, the baptism of the golden fire from heaven. Then the new golden age will have come.

The blessing of the Almighty, the Great White Spirit, is with you now . . .

SUBJECT INDEX

———

SPIRITUAL UNFOLDMENT 1
WHITE EAGLE

*How to discover the Invisible Worlds and
Find the Source of Healing*

The aim of the first volume in the SPIRITUAL
UNFOLDMENT series is to show how by spiritual
unfoldment man can truly contact the higher
spiritual realms and so comprehend the fulness
of life. It makes plain a simple, tried course of
spiritual unfoldment which is based on practice,
not on theory. It also illuminates the subject of
spiritual healing, showing the source from which
it comes, and the laws attendant upon it.

137 + vii pp, hardback
ISBN 0–85487–012–1

SPIRITUAL UNFOLDMENT 2
WHITE EAGLE

The Ministry of Angels and the Invisible World of Nature

White Eagle takes the reader into the inner world and reveals the hidden life within the nature kingdom. He describes in fascinating detail the fairies and elemental beings who, under the command of the angels, help to make the world beautiful and productive for human kind by their work with all growing things. He speaks of the angels and their work with man, from those whose glory and purpose is almost beyond our finite comprehension right down to the least, not far removed from the fairies themselves.

The panorama of life White Eagle unfolds, and the order and purpose inherent in it, reveal his own deep knowledge and experience. But as always, truth is expressed in simple human terms which all can understand. This is one of White Eagle's most valuable books, for knowledge of and co-operation with this inner world of nature can bring the greatest happiness to man.

103 + xi pp, hardback
ISBN 0–85487–001–6